Published by the Penguin Group
Penguin Books Ltd, 80 Strand, London WC2R 0RL, England
Penguin Group (USA) Inc., 375 Hudson Street, New York, New York 10014, USA
Penguin Group (Canada), 90 Eglinton Avenue East, Suite 700, Toronto, Ontario,
Canada M4P 2Y3 (a division of Pearson Penguin Canada Inc.)
Penguin Ireland, 25 St Stephen's Green, Dublin 2, Ireland
(a division of Penguin Books Ltd)
Penguin Group (Australia), 250 Camberwell Road, Camberwell, Victoria 3124,
Australia (a division of Pearson Australia Group Pty Ltd)
Penguin Books India Pvt Ltd, 11 Community Centre, Panchsheel Park,
New Delhi – 110 017, India
Penguin Group (NZ), 67 Apollo Drive, Rosedale, North Shore 0632,
New Zealand (a division of Pearson New Zealand Ltd)
Penguin Books (South Africa) (Pty) Ltd, 24 Sturdee Avenue, Rosebank,
Johannesburg 2196, South Africa

Penguin Books Ltd, Registered Offices:
80 Strand, London WC2R 0RL, England
www.penguin.com

First published 2009
1
Copyright © Take That, 2009
The moral right of the authors has been asserted
For further permissions see pages 206-207

Printed and bound by Firmengruppe APPL, aprinta druck, Wemding, Germany
Colour reproduction by Altaimage
A CIP catalogue record for this book is available from the British Library
ISBN: 978-0-718-15579-7

Where directional symbols appear throughout this book, reference is being
made to a spread that either precedes or succeeds the text depending on
the direction of the arrow

www.greenpenguin.co.uk

Penguin Books is committed to a sustainable future
for our business, our readers and our planet.
The book in your hands is made from paper
certified by the Forest Stewardship Council.

TAKE THAT / TAKE TWO

I was looking at the premiere as just a chance for
me to say thank you to people from first time round.
It felt like an end for me, not a beginning.

GARY _____ We were at the Coronet cinema in Notting Hill and
the big joke was that we couldn't even get a West End
cinema to screen the documentary. The whole night felt
like it was going to be a disaster. We didn't look like a
band when we met up again, so Mark and his manager,
Jonathan, who went on to become our manager, were
gathering clothes together with a stylist. I'd been to
London the week before shopping with Patrick Cox
for something to wear for the screening. I hadn't bought
clothes for about four years and I'm rubbish at it, but
Patrick helped me to buy a load of stuff from Selfridges.
Back in the day I would've asked Mark to help, but the
fact was I didn't know him that well any more. Jonathan
and the stylist matched the lads' suits and ties to what
I'd bought with Patrick.

We all had a feeling of doom and worry, that
impending fear of looking like a bunch of losers. The
documentary felt like we were going to be exposed
again. Even the introduction to it was more of a speech
about Simon Cowell's production company, which had
made it, than it was about Take That. But within two
minutes there were old shots of us on *Lorraine Kelly*
and the like and everyone was in stitches. After ten,
fifteen minutes there was a sense that everyone was
actually enjoying it. We stayed the whole night and
went to the after-show party, which Nigel had always
told us not to do as a band first time round. But we were
so buzzed by the reaction to the screening it was as if
we'd resorted to being back in the 90s. It was actually
bloody brilliant.

MARK _____ I was looking at the premiere as just a chance for
me to say thank you to people from first time round.
It felt like an end for me, not a beginning. Little did
we know. You know I worked out that probably that
first week we all got together was when Emma became
pregnant with our son Elwood, so it was a new chapter
on many levels.

JASON _____ I was a wreck at the screening of our documentary. It was the end of 2005. I felt a lot of revulsion about everything. I was so unsure of what I was doing there and it was a horrible day. I was stony-faced with absolute fear and totally bewildered by it all. I was just saying to the lads all the way through the day leading up to it, 'I can't do this.' Our old manager, Nigel, was there and I couldn't look at him. It was a very tense time for all of us, but I felt it the worst. That night the promoter Simon Moran whispered in all of our ears individually about doing a comeback show. I had no idea whether it was the right or wrong thing to do. I was in no-man's land.

HOWARD _____ Surprisingly there were at least fifty fans there, which was about fifty more than I'd expected to turn up, so I'd taken a lot of friends and family along for moral support. There were a lot of laughs going round when the film was on, but none of us had any idea that this was the launch pad for something new. It was very smart of Simon to spot the potential there. Jay hated every minute of it. He was uncomfortable about fans and the press being there. But I really did enjoy the documentary itself.

GARY _____ I'm always the first ready before we go on stage. I'll be in full regalia while the others are still showering. Mark always cleans his teeth before performing, which I find a bit weird. We'll have a bit of music on. Howard will put on some stuff that's got no vocals that you've never heard of, cool as anything, and everyone will complain so I'll stick on a bit of Booty Luv. We've never had our own dressing rooms and we don't now, which some people find a bit odd but it feels right for us. Everyone leaves us alone for a good forty minutes to get ready before stage time. It's lovely, a sacred time for us, the calm before the storm.

JASON ———————— The documentary had screened in December 2005 and we were back rehearsing by February 2006. It felt good again. The tour kicked off in April. We'd got the first few nights out of the way, got the reviews in, the crowd were on side and we were feeling on top of it all in a very short amount of time.

GARY —————————— There's always a little high-five before we go on stage to make all the family feel together. Before the shows on the comeback tour we'd do the hokey-cokey with all the band and the dancers. We love all the personnel to join us on stage. We love becoming that bigger thing – the touring group. I love that little part of people's lives that you're having an effect on. You can tell they're not just there for the money, it's about being part of something they genuinely enjoy.

GARY —————— We were nowhere near in our stride at this point of
the comeback. If we were going to do a video next
week we'd all know what to expect. We'd be all 'We
need a bigger van and an iPod dock! How can we work
in these conditions!' But it was all very new again at
this point. But I was so certain of the track I was in a
good mood. I'd had so many good reactions from the
people I'd played 'Patience' to. I had a suspicion it
was going to be enormous, so I was a bit like 'Oh, who
cares what the video's like'. I was feeling good about it.
But I had no idea what it would do for our careers.
We'd all seen bands coming back and I think the one
thing it's impossible to underestimate is that first piece
of original work that you release.

It's the life or death of the situation. You get it
wrong and you're just a band that can sell a few dates
and go through the old stuff. 'Patience' was the first
proper piece of the jigsaw of us coming back. We wrote
it between the stadium and arena dates of the comeback
tour, and it was one of the first things we did for the
record, which is unbelievable, really. I'd had the title for
ages. George Michael had had an album called *Patience*,
but I couldn't think of a song with that name. If we
could get a song with a connection to it, it felt like a
great word to connect with us coming back. If you listen
to the music of the song it sounds like a big celebration
but the lyric isn't, which kind of worked even better
for our comeback.

Usually songs are about either starting or ending
a relationship, you rarely get songs about that middle
ground. It felt we were really onto something that hadn't
been nailed in song before, which is the Holy Grail as
a songwriter. Even writing it was an amazing point.

GARY —————————— We were all dreading the 'Patience' video shoot.
We couldn't quite imagine what it'd feel like to shoot
a video again with the four of us after all those years.
And we were all pleasantly surprised. The director
was so quick. Usually you'll do ten shots and pick the
best but he'd go for the shot and say, 'Right! Brilliant!
Next!' We were all shot individually. Mark's call time
was 5.30 a.m, Howard's was 7.30 a.m., Jay's was
10.30 a.m. and I was three in the afternoon. I got the
lie-in. I got up, had me breakfast, went shopping, had
me lunch and was even cheeky enough to be a bit late.
Just to rub salt in it.

HOWARD —————————— By the time we'd finished the song we loved it and by
the time we'd finished the video we loved that, too, and
you can't ask more from a comeback than that. There
was a sense even when we were shooting it that it was
going to be a great video. Gary had put a confidence
in me about this song because he's such a confident
person. He's always sure that a tour will sell out and
we're always sitting in the back saying 'No it won't.'

JASON _____ The 'Patience' video was the first time we'd worked with Luke and Liz, our stylist and groomer, who've been with us for the whole thing second time round and done a fantastic job. Luke's been brilliant. Kept it really consistent. He always wants to do his best. He really cares. And when he brings us something that we don't like he looks a little bit gutted. We loved Iceland. We spent all our time in the wild. The landscape was unreal.

HOWARD _____ Camera phones are a big difference this time. They were never there before. They can be a bit of a pain in the arse because not everyone had a camera to hand before and now everyone has one.

MARK —————————— My call time was the early one for the 'Patience' video.
I felt a real responsibility at this point for everyone
else because I'd still been shooting videos during the
quiet years. I felt quite protective towards everyone,
so I said I'd do the first call for the video. I don't feel
that anymore. I don't need to. I wanted to look after
them for those first few months, because I'd been
doing interviews and videos and I knew what everyone's
attitude to them was. I had a bit of the mother in me
in Iceland.

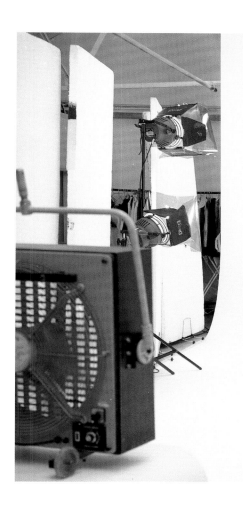

MARK ———————— Luke's such a lovely man. He's a mate first before he's our stylist. He's Mr Cool. He's our age, and he understands and knows us. We built up trust with him very early on, and he's been with us for the whole time since we've been back. Everybody's headed in the same direction, and he's doing a great job with the clothes.

GARY _____ The *Beautiful World* sleeve wasn't a premeditated shoot. We didn't have a cover shot in mind. But we got back to London from Granada and there it was. It was so obvious to all of us that the picture of the four of us against the yellow was the cover of the comeback album.

JASON ——————— We went to shoot the *Beautiful World* sleeve in Granada, Spain, and had a great time doing it. The album cover was meant to be shot on the roof of a building. Tom, the photographer, was really excited by the shot, then some girl came along and got the authorities to shift us off because we didn't have permission to be up there. The light was great and the shot was perfect but this girl was having none of it. In the end it worked out for the best, because if we hadn't got kicked off we never would've got the shot we ended up with, which we were all so happy with.

MARK ——————— The *Beautiful World* album was the first time the four of us had ever been into the studio to write together, and we had no idea how it was going to work out. I remember us having a conversation about what type of record we wanted to make and, because we were all getting on a bit, we thought it might be slightly inappropriate to dig out the lycra and codpieces again.

GARY —————————— Tom's more of a rock-band photographer. But I loved what he did with the imagery for us for *Beautiful World*. Somehow it works now. Obviously it would never have done in the past.

JASON —————————— We all came back with big hair. We'd call each other the Hair Bear Bunch.

GARY —————————— Jay just won't let it go, will he? When he's forty he's got to leave it behind. He can't walk down the street without cracking a move off.

JASON —————————— Every now and again I'll do a handstand. Just to get the blood into my head and to practise balance. And to show off. Get them all jealous.

GARY —————— I found out later that my old music teacher from
school actually lives in the town we did the shoot
in. It was such a shame I didn't know at the time
because everyone would've loved him. He was a
really off-the-wall character.

GARY ——————— I could tell Mark didn't want to do the first shot on Bryan's shoot. There's a moment at the start of every shoot when you get the tone of the day, and I did think, 'What are we in for here, then?' But the rest of the day was brilliant. Mark didn't like the idea of spelling out 'love' but it came out perfectly. I think Mark wanted to spell it differently or something and I was like, 'Please don't let's start the day like this.' But it turned out great.

JASON ——————— When I say we all hate photo shoots, you can take that back for this one. It was Bryan Adams shooting us and we had a ball. We loved it. It's the most entertaining shoot we've ever done. He'd set up so much apparatus and props and he just snapped away while we were behaving like we were on an adventure playground. He's very highly regarded in the photographic world and you can see how that works. He must be so used to being shot himself that he knows how boring shoots can be. So he just uses his imagination. We didn't have to just tolerate it, we actually had fun that day.

JASON —————— I haven't really got a big complex about him, but
Howard looks brilliant here. He's got the soul of Joe
Cocker. He isn't really my rival, though. Honest.

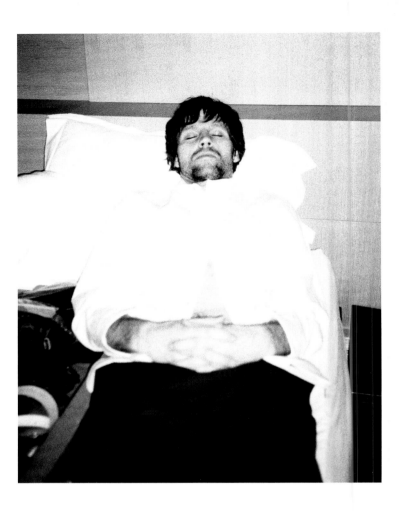

JASON ——————— This picture's on my wall and it's one of all our
favourites. It's supposed to look like *The Rat Pack* or
Ocean's Eleven or whatever, but what I particularly love
about it is that we're not playing poker, we're playing
snap. It's Howard's go and Gary's just got it. Brilliant.

GARY ——————— It was nice being shot by another artist. I'd met him
before and really liked Bryan Adams. He's a nice bloke
and he's a worker. Jonathan got the picture framed for
all of us for Christmas. It's on my wall.

HOWARD ——————— There's a seriousness about winning in Jay's eyes, even
if we are only playing snap. I can see it. I know that
man's face so well. He's laughing along with it but,
actually, he wants to win. The position of his hand, the
look in his eyes, he's on the ball and he wants to win.

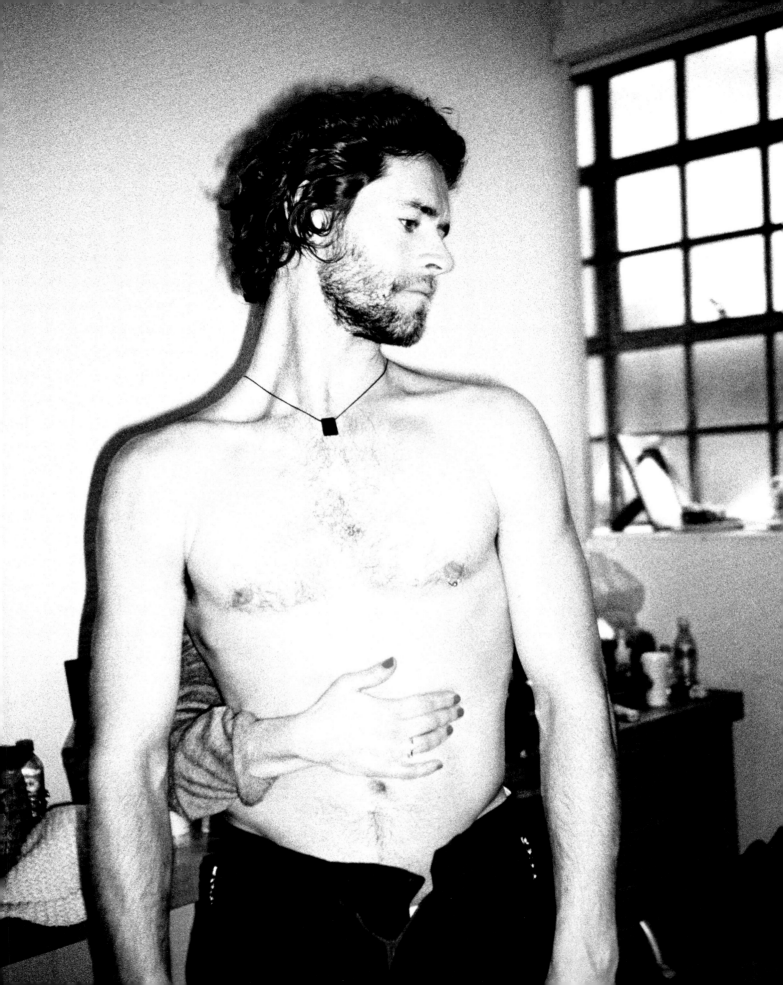

GARY ———————— The entrance to MTV Italy is practically next to an Italian sort of BHS and a WH Smith. It's literally just off the shopping precinct. We had to walk round and there's always a bit of fuss. In Italy if one person stands and stares everyone joins in. The whole street can get excited if someone spots George Clooney.

JASON ———————— We were thicker skinned the first time round, because it felt natural and we all really did want to be famous. We took it in our stride. There was a youthful cockiness to it all, which we don't have any more. There's a slight sense of embarrassment to some of the reportage of me this time, and it's always in this kind of situation when fans are gathering.

MARK —————— There's a certain mindset and sense of anticipation before going on to any stage. It's like going off to war for half an hour. There's another sense here of 'What the hell are we doing back in Japan as Take That?' Almost ten years later we had to find our position again as a band and how our dynamic worked within it.

JASON —————————— Everything about the comeback felt so different and getting the *GQ* Men of the Year award wasn't the end of it. We were invited to the *Q* Magazine Awards. The *GQ* team was really easy to be around. The writer Alex was a good bloke and the photographer Hamish was brilliant. It just felt so different from what had happened with Take That stage one. Those magazines wouldn't have touched us first time around. Tokyo's like a different planet, which I always like.

GARY _____ Like any other photoshoot, the one in Japan was not enjoyable for me. We've tried hard over the years to make them more enjoyable, but they're just not. Unless you're absolutely obsessed with yourself I can't see how you could enjoy being sat on the side of a road in Roppongi, Tokyo for half an hour while someone points a lens at you. It's something I've never got used to. The trip was weird because we hadn't travelled that far from England this time round. What started as a six-week trip we slowly managed to whittle down to a week in Japan and a week in Australia. It pretty much finished me off with long haul for the band. Three of us have got children now, and I was really homesick.

MARK ——————— Gaz was really nice to me about 'Shine' going to number one while we were out in Japan. He said, 'You must be so proud of yourself, and you should be.' And, yes, I was, but it was more of a sense of relief for me. It was more 'thank God'. Everyone knew that 'Patience' would be massive. We all had a feeling about it. But 'Shine' was very different from what Take That had been before; it was so removed from what we were that there was a huge sense of relief when it hit number one.

GARY ——————— Japanese radio stations like you to go in and sing a cappella, so we did 'Patience' with Jay playing the guitar. It felt a little bit like starting all over again. Part of me was thinking, 'Brilliant, let's see how much difference we can make in a week here.' And another part was thinking, 'I can't be arsed.' It wasn't a great week for us, to be honest, but something great did happen back home while we were away. It was the week that 'Shine' went to number one in the UK. We went up to the bar on the top floor of the Hyatt Hotel, which I made sure we were staying at after seeing it in the film *Lost in Translation*, and celebrated being number one.

Even though 'Shine' was a band thing, it was Mark's triumph. It was a massive moment for him. He'd had a lot of rejection as a solo artist. My solo failures were very public, but he'd tried it ten times. I tried once and he kept going. So what a day that was for him. It was very important for him.

JASON ——————— I remember having a conversation with the writer and photographer from *GQ* in the dressing room about who'd win out of a hundred men and a lion. I said the lion. But everybody else disagreed and thought a hundred men would win, which I still refuse to believe.

GARY —————— Howard hates doing interviews. He just hates them and it's because he's shy. As time's gone on we're not so likely to be forced to do something we don't like doing, which is a great situation to be in. That's why there are four of us. He gets so uncomfortable in an interview. He'll start daydreaming during them. The poor lad always gets paired up with me so I do all the talking. I can talk for England.

HOWARD ———————— I've never liked being interviewed. I just don't have the confidence to be one of four or, even worse, one of five. One on one I can handle in an interview and I'll do OK with it, but when it comes to a group situation I find it very difficult to speak up. It's just a confidence thing, really.

JASON _____ We consult between the four of us about everything this time round. Everything's discussed more and it's a lot more democratic. We'll all take our own turns and everyone listens to everything each of us has to say. We don't argue much, but we can bicker, particularly Mark and me. When it's crossed words with Howard or Gary it's a different thing, but with Mark we're like two old women.

GARY —————— We communicate very well in our time off, and there's a lot of mutual understanding because of our shared history. We'll accompany Mark on one of his fag breaks and in that ten minutes we will get a ton of stuff sorted. It's very rare that we're split on things. We don't dress anything up because we've known each other for so many years, which makes Take That a very easy band to be in. For big decisions that you'd think might be fraught with indecision, it is remarkably easy. It's just a decision made between four people.

GARY ——————— They've got a Harrods and a Signature Lounge at Luton airport and we'll find ourselves in that lounge quite a lot for short-haul trips to Europe. Luton's actually quite a flash airport. When movie stars fly in from the States they all land at Luton. I believe it's something to do with the length of the runway. At the other airports for private planes, like Farnborough, the runways aren't long enough. So Luton ends up getting everyone going through. We've spotted quite a few people there. It can be quite social.

GARY _____ *EastEnders* had been in Pinewood studios and were using the water tank the day before we shot the 'I'd Wait for Life' video. Phil Mitchell was drowning after a car smash. The divers were telling us, 'Eh, eh, it's all go this week. Had those *EastEnders* in yesterday.' We had a day swimming round in the tank. It was a bit of an odd video. The end shot was of us all on bits of plane wreckage. It was about the time the show *Lost* had just come out. That was the reference. But it made no sense to the song whatsoever.

JASON ——————— Kim Gavin, our Tour Director, has been with us since the first tour first time round and he's still with us now. We call him our fifth member. We couldn't do the shows without him. Any ideas we have he can make work for the stage and he brings his own great ideas along, too.

MARK ——————— Rehearsals are never my favourite part of the process. But there's always something comforting about it being the same set up that it was ten years before, with Kim in the middle discussing ideas.

GARY ——————— I wanted an upright piano for 'Shine' on the tour because I always have grands, which can look a bit old-fashioned. We bought this piano off eBay and decorated it with the mirrors, but it was an idea that didn't go anywhere in the end. I don't even know where it is now. There will be loads of little details like that going into the preparation of our shows because they are so key to our audience. We take so much care with them. You don't want anyone leaving a Take That show feeling they've not had value for money, and that takes a lot of time and energy to perfect.

HOWARD ——————— It's a very weird time when you're putting a tour together. By this stage you're just wondering how these things are really going to work. How will it all come together? But it all happens in the end.

JASON _____ Howard knew he was going to get centre stage in the rehearsals for the *Beautiful World* tour which explains why he's wearing his favourite tracksuit. I've got my shit tracksuit on because I've been banished to the back.

HOWARD —————— I still have waves of insecurity on stage. What am I doing here? But I've got so much more confidence this time than I ever had before.

MARK —————— The *Beautiful World* tour was such a big challenge after the *Greatest Hits*. The idea of topping that on an emotional level was pretty much impossible so we had to ramp everything else up. We made it a little bit more theatrical, starting off as presidents on the platform. We tried to make it a bit more established and spectacular.

JASON ——————— Jonathan, our manager, had managed Mark through his solo years so there was a good rapport between the two of them. They bicker like old women, but when they're having a laugh it's just lovely to watch. They grew up together back in Oldham. We knew him from the first time round and I always thought of him as a quiet lad, quite shy and pensive. He'd come along to the shows back in the old days. He went to law school and got his qualifications and, coupled with the fact that he'd managed Mark, we just knew he'd be the perfect candidate. It was like he'd accidentally served an apprenticeship with Mark. He was a friend and a fan of the band in the 90s.

MARK ——————— Getting Jonathan in as our manager was a big thing for me. Obviously I trusted him because I'd known him for so long and worked with him a lot, but the fact was that the lads took him to their heart, too.

GARY —————————— Jonathan was at our very first gig Take That ever played in Huddersfield and has a big history with us. He's such an integral part of the band now it's as if it was always meant to be. Mark and Jonathan are always laughing at my clothes. Fittings will always be going well until Luke, our stylist, starts dressing me. I hate fittings. If I've been training and Luke comes and nothing fits, then it's a great day. 'Oh, you'd better take those in!' But the other side of this is that if he comes and nothing fits, I go home a bit miserable because everything's too small.

I go up and down in weight like nobody's business. I can be four or five pounds heavier from one day to the next. It never works itself out. So fittings are always a bit of a dread. Howard can put any item of clothing on and look brilliant, while I'm always last to be fitted. But I'm not looking for sympathy.

HOWARD —————————— Jonathan is always smiling and laughing. We have no idea how much work he does behind the scenes. But we know it's a lot. And most importantly, we know that he's one of us.

JASON —————— For 'Never Forget' on the last tour we had a section where loads of famous iconic historical figures walked interactively through a screen: John Lennon, Charlie Chaplin. This was Audrey Hepburn, who was played very admirably by one of our dancers, Princess. She's actually called Laura, but we all call her Princess. She did a great job with it.

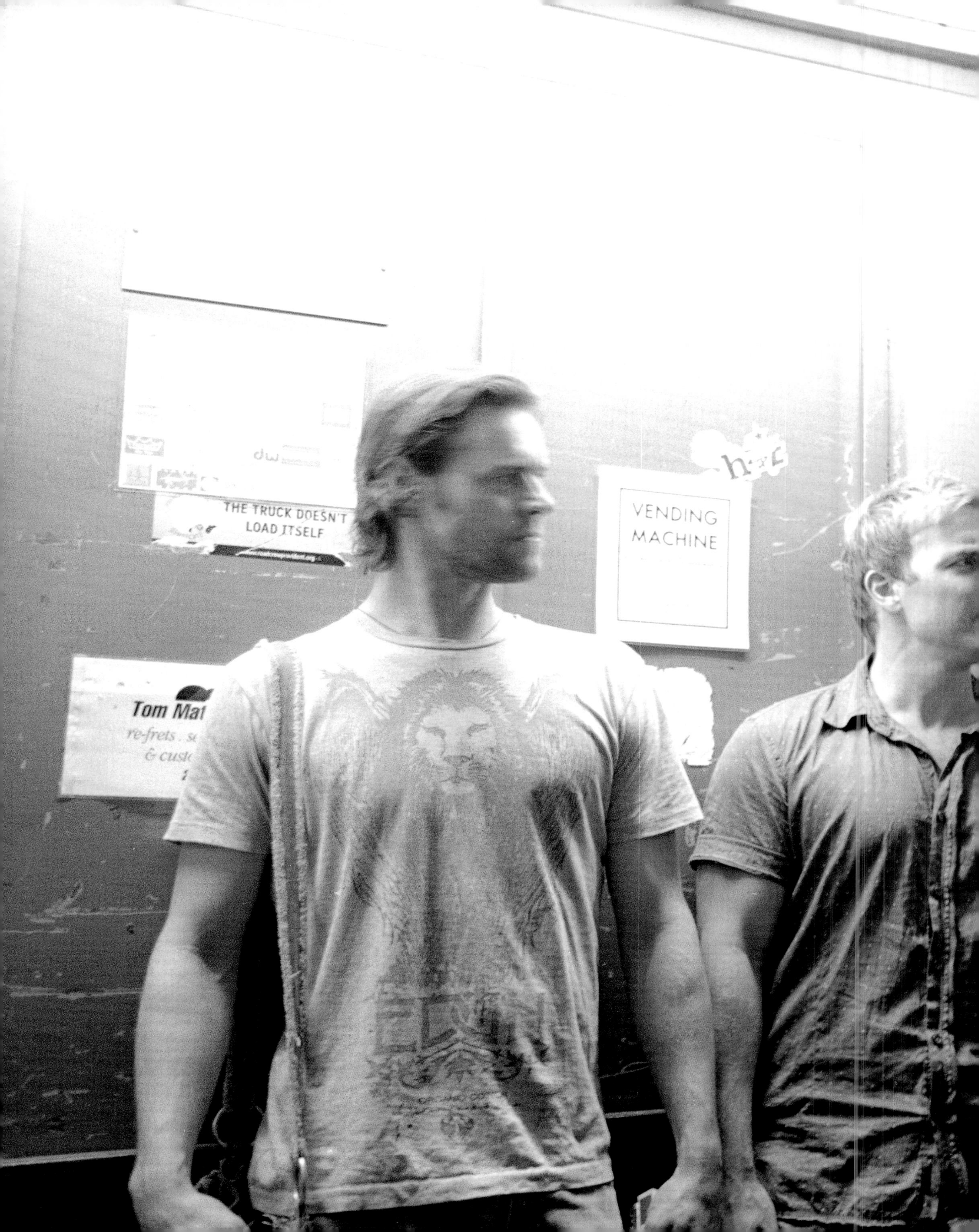
THE TRUCK DOESN'T
LOAD ITSELF
VENDING
MACHINE

MARK —————— There were a million ideas for the 'Rule the World' video. At one point we were supposed to be going up to Jodrell Bank to be filmed on the satellite dishes. The simple idea was best. It's a song that we're so proud of. We'd sung some melodies into a mobile phone that made up the start of the song. We went to see the film, and almost within a day we'd delivered it to the director. I'd done my first solo record at Abbey Road and it always feels like going back home to me.

GARY —————————— We love Abbey Road, Studio One. We've done all our string sessions there since 'Back for Good'.

JASON —————————— 'Rule the World' is definitely the biggest single of the comeback, though ironically it never got to number one and stalled at number two for ever. It's the biggest song we do live, too, and always goes down the best. We filmed the video at Abbey Road, Studio One. I just don't like cameras in front of me, full stop. I love the attitude of bands like Radiohead and Arctic Monkeys, where there's so little of them around visually. But our band is such a different thing. Take That is about our faces and personalities, and you have to accept that the visuals are very important for the kind of band we are.

HOWARD —————————— Me and Jay have always had a laugh together. We still do. And the 'Rule the World' video was such a good one to make. 'Rule the World' has taken over from 'Back for Good' as our signature song. Every time I hear it on a sports tournament or for the football or for anyone winning anything it always makes me buzz. The end of the song is just brilliant. 'All the stars are coming out tonight'. It's just a great line.

MARK ——————— The *Brit Awards* is like the Christmas office party for us now. The girlfriends and wives come along. We all have a drink together. Most of the time I am thinking, 'How the hell did this happen again?' or 'We don't deserve this', but now and again it's OK to be proud.

GARY ——————— We have the same attitude to award ceremonies as most people, which is that they're a very good advert for your records. But on this occasion when we'd come back, we hoped to win the public award for 'Shine' but the live award just floored us. It was one of those brilliant feelings. We always used to go to those things with a fear that a rock band would take the piss out of us, but we actually felt a part of it that time. We felt like we'd actually arrived.

HOWARD ———————— We've never won best album at the *Brits* and I don't think we ever will. The industry vote for it and they tend to be people who come from a rock rather than a pop background. So I guess these awards mean more to us than they do to rock bands, because they're expected to win them. I'm sure it means nothing to a band like Coldplay, but to us it means a lot because the industry isn't weighted towards pop. That acceptance has happened this time round, though. The first time we went back to the *Brits* we walked from our seats to the stage and everyone was looking at us and it wasn't suspicious any more.

Everyone actually looked chuffed for us, which meant a lot to me. I felt like we'd proved something. I thought, 'We're back, we're bigger than ever and we've actually pulled this off.' I think everyone sitting round those tables was thinking the same thing. People can say what they like about the music, but they can't say anything about the achievement and the luck that's joined together this time round.

JASON ——————— We are absolutely shit at accepting awards. It always goes wrong. We just can't be witty and incisive and funny and entertaining at that moment. We've had a BBM about it. We just bumble. We try too hard and you get this weird feeling of false modesty from us, which is so far from what we're thinking. It makes me cringe. I don't know what it is. People tend to do it two ways: this is cool, thanks, a bit of modesty; or they get up and imply they deserve it, which can be a bit hideous. With us, we get painfully shy about accepting awards. We should just be gracious, but there's still something in us that makes us feel like we don't deserve it. We need to sharpen up. We never prepare anything.

HOWARD ——————— I do have a terrible habit of going on my computer during meetings. I'm always listening to dance music and downloading it when everyone's asking me to make a really important decision. I'm on Beatport getting music together and burning it onto CDs. The DJ thing is still important to me. It's my thing away from the band. It's important to keep my sense of identity this time, too, away from what the band is. I love what Take That have become again and I love what I give to it, but I love other stuff too and DJing at the weekend is part of that for me.

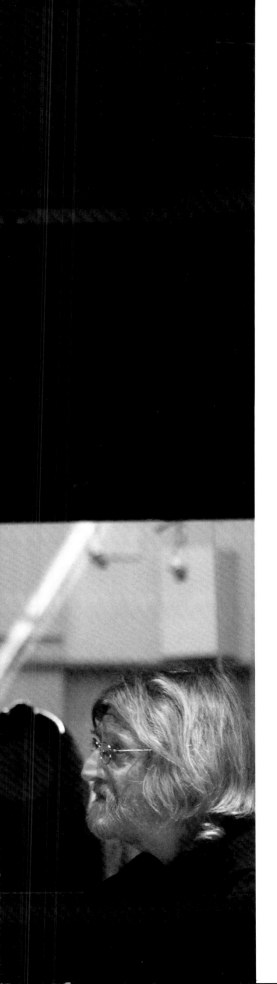

GARY————— Wil Malone, our string arranger, has done everything with us since we've come back. He's become a great friend. All those great runs in 'Shine', which make the song so special, he came up with. We were recording *The Circus* at Abbey Road again. I met Wil for a solo album and we kept in touch. He's a brilliant talent and the first call we make when we start an album. He never stops smoking and no one ever tells him he can't either!

JASON ————— Wil's brilliant. He's a genius. Our hero. The string arrangements are a beautiful experience. Gary and Mark are the studio boffins and they'll be much more involved in the architecture of the sound, but it's amazing to be a part of it all happening. It blows me away watching a twenty-four-piece orchestra recording. You'd have to have a heart of stone not to be moved by that.

GARY———————— We recorded some more of *The Circus* at Sarm Studios. Ryan is stood behind me. He's our studio programmer and he goes right the way through with us from demo stage to the finished record. He'll spend the whole album with us. He's our little genius. The studio time really is my favourite, basically.

MARK———————— I could live in the studio, I love writing. Recording can sometimes be a bit boring trying to find the right sound, but the studio is my second home. I have a little one we call the Rabbit Hutch at the bottom of my garden. Every man needs his shed.

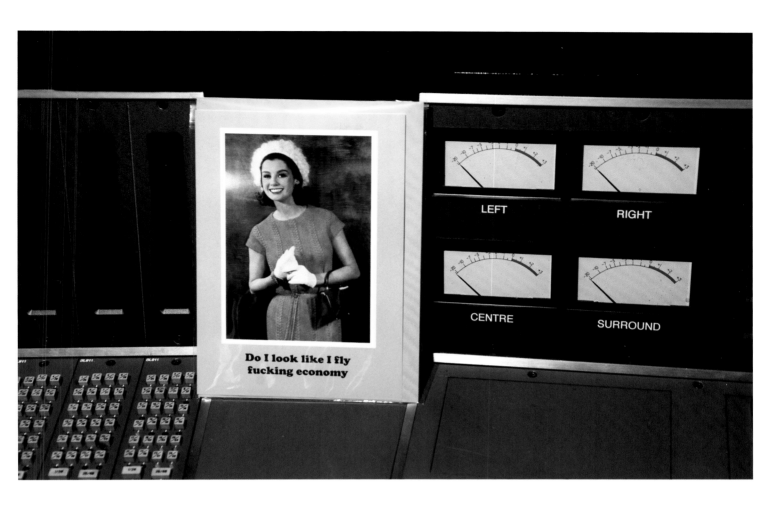

JASON ————— I bought some daft cards from a card shop on Portobello Road. We put one on the mixing desk as we were making *The Circus* and it made everyone laugh. We were booked in there from April–August 2008. Two and a half months writing, two and a half months recording. Jon, the producer, particularly loved the card.

GARY ——————— We still make our albums in quite a traditional way, with those enormous mixing desks. I guess it comes back to giving the audience their money's worth again. It's got to be absolutely as good as we can make it.

JASON ——————— The moment where major decisions are being made in the studio is quite intense. There'll be a big 'yes' or 'no' at the end of each playback.

MARK —————— Shooting the video to 'Greatest Day' was a revelation.
I felt like I was seeing a different performance than
I'd seen from any of us before. Howard, Gaz and Jay
had all stepped up from *Beautiful World*. It was an
eye-opener for me to see the lads giving it so much;
there was no choreography, it just happened. Because
of the bass frequency up there, a load of swallows
gathered round us while we were filming. It felt like a
special day.

JASON —————— The concept for 'Greatest Day' was a cross between
The Matrix and U2 but none of us thought much of
the end result. I've only watched it once since the
first playback. I don't watch much telly so I haven't
even caught it in passing.

HOWARD —————— I felt so much more confident this time round after
Beautiful World. My involvement in it was so much
greater. But something about this video didn't work.

GARY —————— We've never wanted to turn into one of those bands
where the videos just degenerate and the fact was
Greatest Day was shit. Little things like the iTunes
video charts matter to me, and we want to give the
fans the best that we can possibly do. It just didn't
happen here.

GARY————— It is very rare for me to actually like a photo of myself. The day after we'd done the 'Greatest Day' video we had a really long day on La Brea in LA shooting singles sleeves and promo shots. I SMSd this photo to Dawn to remind her how lucky she is… It's one of the only ones of myself I actually like.

MARK ——————— There was so much optimism around the release of *The Circus*. With *Beautiful World* there was a lot of nerves. You can see the optimism in everybody's eyes. We all wanted to be a part of this thing, and we weren't scared of what it was and what it had become second time round.

GARY ———————— We'd found a great photographer for the album cover. He was so helpful and encouraging and it was bloody boiling at the circus school off Ventura Boulevard so it could have been a tricky day. Mark had bought a great big thick 900-quid book and we'd seen a shot on a tightrope with a beautiful sky behind it. That was it. You always want your album cover to stand out. Our label buys up big advertising spots and with *Beautiful World* the background colour of the yellow had really stood out, so we wanted something similar and striking this time. The idea of a blue sky in the middle of winter, when the record came out, was really appealing.

I had to have a little slug of Jack Daniel's before I got on the trapeze. It was just the sheer height of it for me. Terrified.

JASON ——————— Ten years on and Howard's still got it. Bastard.

☐☐
→

HOWARD ——————— Jay's got it, hasn't he? He's a very handsome man. We had a really enjoyable day shooting *The Circus* cover because it felt like mucking about in the beautiful sun in LA. It actually made me like LA. I'd never really felt at home there but the more I go, the more I like it. We shot it at a circus school and all the guys were lovely. I loved the trampoline. Gary was scared of everything.

☐☐
→

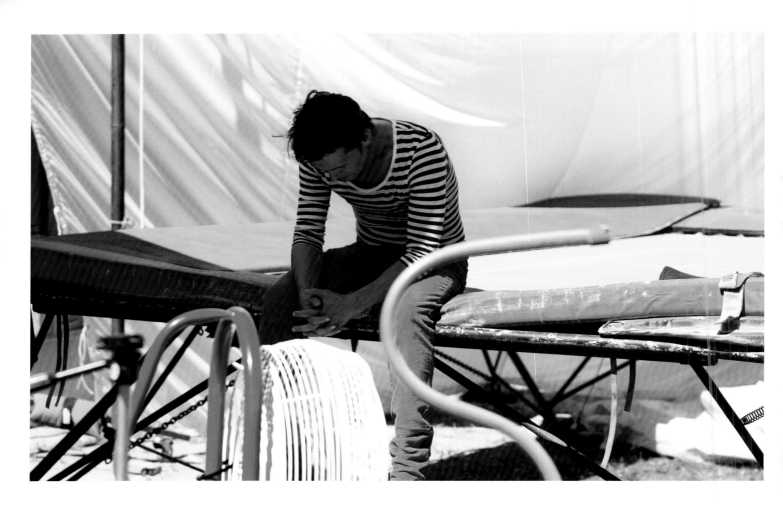

MARK —————— The record company suggested us doing a cover shoot in a studio in London, but I insisted that we did it for real and so, on our last day in LA, we all drove off to this trapeze school. It was the fiercest heat I have ever witnessed and stupidly the night before I had indulged in a few too many glasses of wine. I suffered.

HOWARD —————————— We shot the *Observer Music* magazine cover at the place they film *Dragons' Den*. That didn't excite me so much, but the shoot did. We're trying something, launching the campaign, getting *The Circus* theme in for a major music magazine. It was a great way to kick off the album.

MARK _____

←

The bunting and street-party idea was toyed with for the album cover. The Silver Jubilee is something we all remembered. The fact that everyone who lived on the street came along to it added something to it and you could smell the Britishness of it all: slices of Battenberg cake and sausage rolls. It was the first time we'd played as a band in a video, which is how we'd demoed the song. It was showing a different side of us again and it moves us on a bit. There's a nice community feeling to it.

GARY _____

←

I'd gone off to watch my baby being born, and if you look at the top of the piano you can see my stand-in. We were probably actually giving birth at that exact moment and it's very ironic that the song was called 'Up All Night', given what was happening. The video turned out brilliant. We all remember the Jubilee in 1977 and that looks pretty much exactly like the street that I grew up on. We didn't use any extras at all in the video, just the people from the street. Even though I was only at the shoot an hour, it was a great hour of being in Take That.

JASON —————— I'm a bit gutted the lads didn't tell me what the hat I was wearing for the 'Up All Night' video looked like. It's a bit dustman, a bit tramp, a bit George Formby. We shot the video on a street in Croydon and we invited half the street to come along to it. The houses on the street were just like the ones we all grew up in. It reminded me of Wythenshawe. People were inviting us into their houses for cups of tea between takes, which was lovely. The street party was Mark's idea. He's led the way with ideas for *The Circus*. Songs, videos, tour. In the years he was away, because he was still making albums and doing videos, he'd turned a corner.

He became an artist and he brought it back to the table for us. He'll be in constant contact with Luke about the styling for us. It's doubled our strength as a band. He's such a real asset.

JASON ——————— We rocked at this year's *Brit Awards*, and I loved every
second of it. The outfit was so last minute and Luke
really came through with it. He was our hero that night.
Right up until the start of the show we weren't sure
about wearing the glasses. There was about a minute
to go before the UFO went up and we were saying,
'Do we wear them or not?' We just went all out for it,
and I think it really worked. I got loads of texts from my
family and friends saying it was the best performance
of the night. It's lovely to get those messages, they
mean a lot to me.

GARY ——————— My back was in agony, I felt overweight and I hated the
glasses at this year's *Brits* performance. I know a lot of
people liked it, and the other guys look great, but I
really did feel like a tit. Like Captain Kirk or something.
Because we were on that UFO the technical people
said we couldn't sing live. It was right in front of the
speakers and they said the mics would have fed back.
I felt like a bit of a fraud. I still wish we'd opened the
show!! Never happy!!

MARK ——————— The glasses or no glasses debate went right down to the
wire. Initially we were going to be on a rocket, but it
looked a bit phallic. The initial drawings were basically
of a big knob. The UFO angle was talked about, and
it seemed to work. I liked the glasses, personally,
because I thought they looked a bit Kraftwerk.

JASON —————— The record company in Germany wanted us to release 'The Garden' as the second single from *The Circus* but we weren't keen on the idea. It tanked, so we were probably right. We got some great stills out of the video shoot but the video itself, not so much. Gary looks great, the clothes are brilliant and the imagery works well as stills.

GARY ——————— 'The Garden' shoot was a crap day for me and it really
□ □   isn't one of my favourite videos. What's weird is that
←   it was the same director who did the 'Patience' video,
                   which we'd all loved so much.

HOWARD ——————— I was the first person on set for 'The Garden' and I'd
                   not had a lot of sleep the night before. I decided to try
                   acting the song out. I put myself right into the position
                   of thinking about something sad and I actually got
                   myself into that place. I started welling up at one point
                   and he captured it in the video. I was tired anyway, a
                   bit hung over, I'd just managed to get down a sausage
                   butty and I got to exactly the place where I needed to
                   be for the take. I usually hate having a camera on me
                   like that. They can pick out everything on your face.
                   When you're doing that at 9 a.m. and you've been in
                   make-up since seven in the morning it's sometimes
                   hard, but I really managed to go somewhere here.

GARY ———————— 'The Circus' rehearsals were the most stress-free time we've had preparing for a tour ever. It was very enjoyable the whole way through. We knew what we should be doing and we knew what we wanted to do. Jason can get a bit down on the whole thing. He can have those feelings of not deserving to be there. I don't think he enjoyed the comeback tour. He was working stuff out about what Take That was. But this time he was enjoying every minute of it and he'd found his place within it. I've been writing since I was fifteen and it's like second nature to me.

With Jason, he can feel a bit intimidated, so some of my job now is making everyone feel a part of it. And that's a good job to have. Everyone needs to feel a part of Take That because everyone is a part of it. It makes a happy house and it's so important.

JASON — The unicycles for 'The Circus' tour were Howard's idea. He wanted us to get a skill and everything else was impossible to insure against. We almost didn't get insured for the unicycles. We had to spend a fortune on top of the existing premium. Howard bought us each a unicycle for Christmas. Gary hurt his back preparing for climbing Kilimanjaro, so he had to knock it on the head. We should've been wearing helmets. One of us comes off and that's millions of pounds' worth of tour up in smoke.

MARK — The rehearsals for 'The Circus' tour were a delight. We had the best people working with us, we prepared so well for it and I'm really proud of the result. To do three tours in three and a half years feels like an amazing achievement.

JASON ——————— We're a proper band now, but the clock in the
☐☐
→
background is a good little reminder of where we came
from. You have to be able to appreciate those things
and laugh about them. Deptford John, the guitar tech,
put that up for a bit of a joke. And it is funny.

GARY ——————— That bloody clock finds itself in the most unusual places.
☐☐
→

JASON _____ I get really soppy on tour. The dancers, the musicians,
I just want to hug them all after I've had a couple of
drinks. You don't see them until the next tour or
maybe not ever again, and they do such a wonderful
job. You feel like you're privileged to be around so
many talented people. You get very attached. It's
intimate. 'The Circus' tour was a really enjoyable
rehearsal period.

HOWARD _____ I've always been very impressed by dancers. I respect
them. I've always been a bit conscious of what they're
thinking of us stood around the side. Do they think
we're serious about this? That's another insecurity to
me. But dancing professionally was the thing I wanted
to do and it's the thing I bring to the band. I want to
be respected for it by the people who are brilliant at it.

GARY ———————— We used to do the big pop show in Germany *Wetten, dass..?* in the 90s. It was the one to get. It's a seven-hour live show so you do wonder at what point the audience switches over to watch *Casualty*, or whatever the German equivalent is. We walked into the studio and looked at the set and said to each other, 'So, we're doing "The Garden", then?'

JASON ———————— If 'The Garden' couldn't be a hit after that TV show it was never going to be.

GARY —————— With *The Circus* album the singles have been a bit of a puzzle. 'Greatest Day' was obviously the first and we'd decided that 'Said It All' should be third and released around the time of the tour, but the problem was nailing the second single. The 'Up All Night' video had been a disaster for me because it was the only day we were working in January, and Dawn went into labour while it was being made with our third child so I had to disappear after an hour. With the 'Said It All' video, I made sure I put the hours in and we were all very happy with the result. It was just the four of us, going for it. It put the top hat on *The Circus*.

We came up with the idea over a couple of bottles of wine on a plane home from Italy, which is always the best way. I think all of us will be happy if we never see another clown again, mind. Britney Spears came back with a Circus tour, we were doing one. That's quite enough of clowns now, thank you.

MARK ——————— I always look at where we started off and how much
we've moved on. I think it's funny that we're clowns
in the video because, most of the time, that's how we
see ourselves.

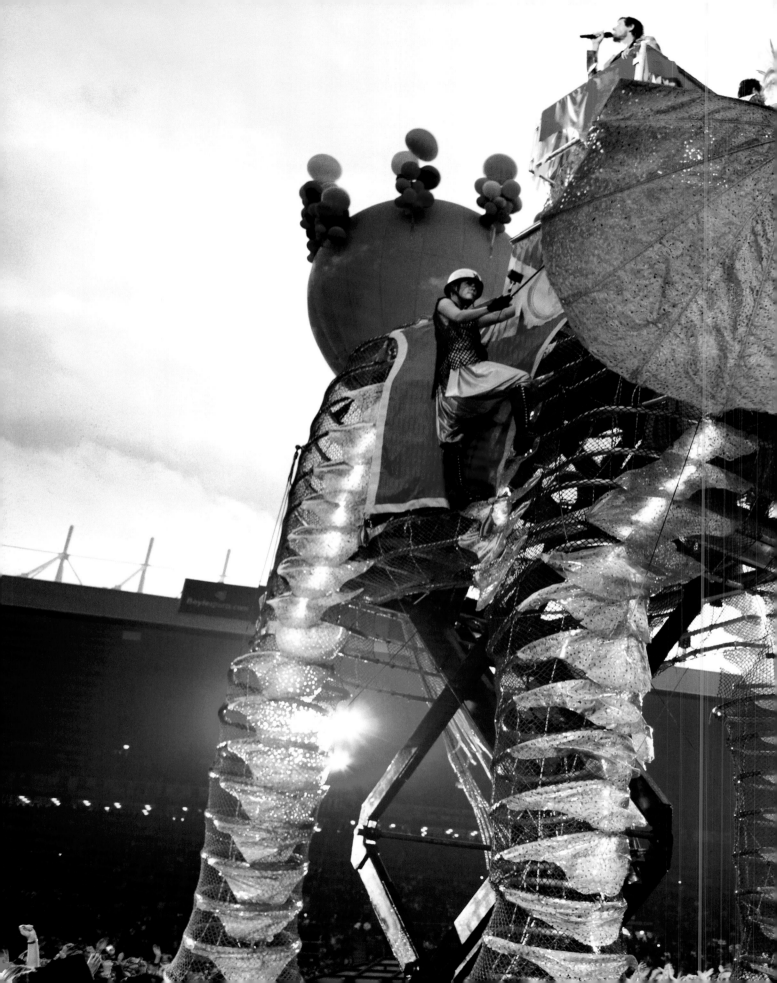

TAKE TWO / INDEX

	Location	Photography

Cover photograph by Jason Bell
Commentary transcribed by Paul Flynn
Book design and direction by Studio Fury
in association with Jonathan Wild, 10 Management
Take That would like to thank all contributing photographers

*Video directed by Sean De Sparengo